CHURCH RUINS.

BY THE

REV. ALEXANDER MACLEOD, D.D.,

AUTHOR OF "CHRISTUS CONSOLATOR," "OUR OWN LIVES THE
BOOKS OF JUDGMENT," ETC.

LONDON:
W. TWEEDIE & CO. (LIMITED), 337, STRAND.

Price One Penny.

"Our holy and beautiful house, where our fathers praised Thee, is burned up with fire: and all our pleasant things are laid waste."—ISAIAH lxiv. 11.

The following Discourse,—the Annual Sermon of the National Temperance League,—was preached in the Metropolitan Tabernacle, London, Sunday, April 18th, 1875, to an immense congregation. The Directors of the League having expressed a desire for its publication, and Dr. Macleod having given his cordial assent, the Publishers have pleasure in issuing it in this form.

June, 1875.

LONDON: BARRETT, SONS AND CO., PRINTERS, SEETHING LANE.

CHURCH RUINS.

IN fulfilling their great function of warning God's people, the prophets often pourtray the future as already present. While no sign yet breaks on the outward eye, they disclose the destruction to which the errors or neglects of the present are sure to lead.

The holy and beautiful house which Isaiah speaks of was still standing. Its destruction was not accomplished for more than a generation after. But in the vivid foresight of the prophet it is already in ruins. He sees the effect in the cause : the future outward material ruin in the deterioration of life and practice which were working to bring it about.

In the same way, long after, our Lord forebodes the destruction of Jerusalem. The city had more than recovered its ancient splendour. But underneath all the splendour the Lord saw only the beginnings of desolation. Everywhere His eye penetrated to ruin. The temple worship, the spiritual and social life, were already in ruins. Far behind, in the past, were the years when pure faith, sincere worship, and righteousness between man and man possessed the life of the people. Here at His feet lay the hypocrisy, the unrighteousness, the neglect of the poor, He had so often to lament and reprove. These were the ruins He saw. It was over these, when He beheld the city, that He lifted up His voice and wept.

The Bible is full of this pathetic foresight, this prevision of approaching woe. Some evil is at work, some error has begun to spread, some vice, or wrong-doing, in social life is suffered to remain ; and God's people are negligent, or asleep, or indifferent, and straightway a loud note of warning is struck by God's prophet, and forward on the pathway of the Church is projected a vision of disaster and ruin.

It is such a note I desire to strike to-day. I wish to arrest the Christian conscience on the general attitude of Church-going people to the great evil of Intemperance. I wish also to suggest that the continuance of that attitude is fraught with peril to the Church itself, and is even now a sign and source of decay in the life and influence of every church in the land.

And I think nowhere so fitly as in England may such a note of warning be sounded. Of nearly three parts out of four in our country, the footprints of the past are ruins of churches. They are the ruins of the cathedrals, abbeys, priories, and chapels, of the Church that was once the Church of this whole land. What wrought that ruin? What broke down those walls? It needed some strong force on walls like these to work such ruin. With what an impress of strength they still rise from the ground! How grandly they spread themselves in their broken masses over the sites they cover! Pass into one of the ruined churches. The bell-tower soars upward still with a noble bearing to more than half its ancient height. Between those pillars, of which only the bases now remain walked the procession of priests and religious men in the olden time. From that great window streamed down on them the orient morning; far up among those corridors and arches floated the psalms they chanted as they marched. In that spot stood the altar, in that other the pulpit, and there the baptismal font. And now it is all a ruin. The walls are broken, the windows are empty of their splendours, the roof is gone, the rich carvings have become shapeless knobs of stone, and only fragments remain of what were once the statues of kings and queens.

If we go back among the centuries when all that now carries this stamp of death was astir with life, we shall see a swell and outflow of Church activity which has never been surpassed. We shall hear the great bell ring out again from that empty tower. We shall see the fields all sprinkled with worshippers flocking to its call. Congregations as numerous, as devout as any of the present time shall be seen to fill the church.

What emptied such churches? What touched those beautiful buildings with the hand of death? Is it only a story of storm and winter, of time and death, of one generation coming and another going, of fashions changing, and then the rain and the wind beginning to beat upon the old house until it falls? Believe it not. No once-living Church is allowed in God's world to perish so. Some inner force of ruin, some failure in the life, or some neglect in the work, of the Church existed, or it never could have ended so. And what that inner force of ruin was we have only to open a history of the Middle Ages to see. We shall there see a spectacle of a Church called to do a Church's duty among the people and neglecting to do it. We shall see a Church lifted into the supremest power this earth ever witnessed, and failing to use that power for good. A Church face to face with terrible evils in the life of her people, and leaving those evils to work their will. She that ought to have been their mother left them in the wilderness to perish. She put self-seeking in the place of her Lord, splendour of worship and priestly power in the place of temperance and purity and truth

—and, by her neglect, broke down the everlasting marches between sin and righteousness, between purity and impurity in the life of man. That was the secret of her ruin. Her unfaithfulness destroyed her. And the great Church of the Middle Ages—the Church of our own ancestors,—which at one time rendered noble service to humanity, became a habitation of devils, and a moral and spiritual ruin. And at the Reformation the ruin descended on the very walls she had built.

Whatever other lessons may be written for us in such ruins, of these two there can be no doubt—first, that the ruined walls are but the result of ruined churches, the natural and inevitable outcome of ruin in the life or working of the church ; next, that the inner ruin may be in progress, and all the forces which are to complete it at work, before one speck of decay is visible without. It was so in Isaiah's day ; it was so in the days which preceded the Reformation. The elements of ruin were at work in the thoughts, principles, practices of the churches of those times, and were eating out their life and strength ; and all the while their priests and people were gliding on unconscious of the woe.

It is on these facts I stand to-day. The evil we have to contend with is so gigantic that we can only hope to succeed if the Christian Church is with us in the conflict. And it is very far from being with us. Face to face with this awful sore along every path it treads, and under the most solemn responsibility to take it in hand, it is yet practically all but letting it alone. Can it afford to let it alone ? Can it pass by on the other side and continue itself to prosper ?

Surely I may say that no Christian, or society of Christians, is free to stand aside when questions like these are raised. They mean one stage forward :—What is the worth of the forces in reserve for the Christianising of this land ? They mean one stage back :—Has ruin seized on the Churches of the land ?

Nothing could well come nearer to us, therefore, on an occasion like this, than the question I have raised. I give it a general scope by asking : " What are the things which bring ruin on a Church?"

It is a happy circumstance, in relation to this inquiry, that we are not left to find our reply in the imperfect observation or one-sided inferences of man, but are able to avail ourselves of the teaching of our Lord Himself.

In five of the Epistles to the Seven Churches He has occasion to point out elements of ruin which were at work in those Churches when His message was sent to them, and which did actually work ruin to them in after days. Taking the epistles together, we have a natural history of ruin—or, more precisely, a panoramic exhibition of its successive stages, from the first unsuspected beginnings to the last unmistakable development. We see the first faint touch of decay—the first slight inlet of the destroying force—and then, spot after spot, until the evil has penetrated through the entire life of the Church, and nothing remains but to make manifest to the eye of man what is already a complete ruin before the eye of God.

Taking these Churches in their order, and lifting up what was special to each, we shall find the following conditions set forth as the descending stages in the ruin of Churches :—First. Decay of love to Christ. Second. Decay of pity for human souls. Third. Decay of thoroughness in Christian work. Fourth. Decay of humility.

I.

I think it is very arresting—very well fitted to put all who are interested in the success of an enterprise like ours, and in the welfare of the Church, upon self-examination—that the first element of ruin mentioned is *the decay of love to Christ :* " I have somewhat against thee ; because thou hast left thy first love." The Church to which these touching words were addressed might well receive them with surprise. It was that Church of Ephesus to which Paul's deepest epistle had been sent. It was a Church with a glorious past to look back to. In Paul's day it was full of love—love to Christ, to His people, to His cause ; full of that Divine force which is the one all-conquering power in the war with evil. It was still a zealous Church; it was at one with its Lord in its adhesion to sound doctrine. It held aloft in dark days the banner of truth. It still hated what Christ hated, and it had put His enemies to shame. But along with all this zeal for the truth there was a falling away from love —a declension, not in numbers nor in orthodoxy, but in love. A little thing to look at !—a thing the human eye cannot see, but very patent to the eye of Christ. He, whose own heart is love—who is yearning for love—feels the want of the old fervour—the old out-coming of heart towards Himself. It is not the home which once welcomed Him as its life ; or, if there be welcome still, it has not the old love at its heart. He has occasion to say, as in Jeremiah's days, " I remember the holiness of thy youth, the love of thine espousals, thy walking after me in the wilderness, in a land not sown." That time has gone. A strange new time has come into its place ; and there is this sad want in it—this first touch of woe— this real fall, although only by one step, from life—that the young, fresh, personal love to Christ, stirs no longer at the heart. Other loves may be present, but to want the direct love which goes out upon the Saviour Himself, that is the beginning of ruin for the

Church—the fruitful beginning of neglect in all Christian work. And just that, my Christian friends, is the secret, wherever it exists, of the Church's indifference to the evil which has brought us together to-day. At the root and heart of it lies a failure of love to Christ, and a falling away from sympathy with that yearning sincerity of love in Him which led Him to lay down His life for the lost.

II.

The Churches of Pergamos and Thyatira are those in which the next step in the descent to ruin is exhibited. It begins with conformity to the world; but the deep, underlying evil is *Failure of compassion for human souls*. With the exception of a few Jewish converts, the members had been gathered out of the pagan community. Paganism, therefore, was the world which they had abjured, on which they were not to look wistfully back, from whose influences they were to guard their flock, and to whose beliefs and customs they could no longer conform. And it so happened the test of sincerity with them, as with ourselves, turned on an act of abstinence. The flesh sold in the market was the left portion of animals which had been sacrificed to idols. Could a Christian eat of such flesh? Could he use it without becoming a partaker in idol-worship?

Far more was involved than a scruple of conscience. Mixed up with that whole system of animal sacrifices were customs saturated with impurity and wrong living. They had abandoned those customs; they had come under obligations to forsake "the trespasses and the sins" of the world they had left.

It was a difficult position to maintain. To abstain from flesh offered to idols was to separate from almost the entire social life of the time—to shut themselves out from public and private festivals and hospitalities, and, to that extent, to abridge their undoubted Christian liberty. Yet, in the first fervours of their love, all this had been cheerfully endured. What was animal food, what was the enjoyment of hospitality, when placed in the balance with the salvation of souls?

The two churches had striven to be true to their position; and in many things they had succeeded. There was a maintenance of sound teaching on the central doctrines— "Thou holdest fast my name, and hast not denied my faith." All that! But along with that, there began to be the toleration of loose views regarding practice; and in practice itself, a falling away from the early abstinence; and, in all that, a failure in the concern for human souls.

"Why should we abstain? 'tis such a narrow thing to be an

abstainer.   An idol is nothing, and meat offered to an idol is nothing ; and we are free to enjoy all God's creatures.   Let us cast away our narrowness, and be neighbourly and do as others do, and make no difficulty !"

But it was just the time in the history of those churches when to practise this liberty was to cast stumbling-blocks before the souls of the people.   It was that time which, sooner or later, arises in every mission field, that time of sifting and trial, when old habits begin to reassert their sway, when the converts bend back towards the enjoyments they have left, and recall with a certain longing the self-indulgences of the past.

A generation was springing up who had not themselves known the evils of pagan life,—the children of the first converts.   Instead of being trained up in the fear and hatred of pagan customs, they beheld around them in the Church compliance with, toleration, and at last open defence of, these customs.   Older members repaired to the pagan feasts and ate of the forbidden flesh,—why should young people put a restraint upon their lives ?   They broke loose from the old safeguard and ceased to be abstainers.   They went to the feasts as their neighbours did, they listened to the wild talk, they immersed themselves in the foul atmosphere.   They familiarised their eyes with pagan practices, their ears with pagan songs, and, bit by bit, they were drawn in and down into the pit of unclean life, of utter and abominable wickedness, to which the conformity in the one matter of eating was bait and trap.   The very pathways of the Church became filled with pitfalls; the practices of Church members became the traps and snares.

Do I not seem to be telling a story of the present time ?

That old pagan world is far behind us ; but the world itself is not behind us.   And that with which we are called to contend, is a world with practices as full of danger to the purity and well-being of souls and churches, as any that ever wrought ruin on the earth. And it is still, as in those foul days, a world of self-indulgence and soft living.   The only difference is, that drinking customs have only come into the place of meat offered to idols.   It is when we look at these customs in connection with the evils to which they lead, that we discover that failure of pity for human souls, which is such a portent of evil among the church-going people of our land.   With all the facts brought to light by societies like our own, with all the tragedies disclosed in family histories, with all the witnesses of their evil consequences on our streets, and all the sad fruits of them in our criminal courts, it seems to me that a really strong, earnest, and living Church should be tingling through all its membership with the inquiry: Whether it is not now, as in Pergamos and Thyatira, one of the most immediate and pressing duties of Christian men and women to refuse to conform to customs which are leading to such woes! Be sure, a Church which shuts her eyes on the evil, or folds herself up in her own delights—in mere sermon-hearing, for example, or musical services, or splendid decorations—and is not exercising herself with deep heart-searchings concerning the souls which these customs are destroying, is herself in the very track of ruin. And, therefore, I sound the alarm in the ears of all who have the prosperity of the Church at heart. I avow my own alarm. I am alarmed at the light and chaffy way in which the great Drink Evil is still referred to by members of the Church. I am alarmed at the self-satisfied scorn of abstinence which continues to prevail. I am alarmed at the amount of conformity to the drinking customs which still exists among Christian people; and at the snares and pitfalls opened by this conformity in the very pathways of the Church, in the very habits of her members; and at the awful number of souls which the Church is bound to care for, who are, meanwhile, and by the instrumentality of drink, going down into the abyss.

It is far from my wish to darken a single shadow. There was still much good even in Thyatira, the worst of the two churches—very much activity in works of gentleness and patience. I believe there is also much good, and a real striving after more good, in the churches of our land at present. There are words in the epistle which show that the good members of the church at Thyatira were very good. That is my sincere belief concerning the good members of the churches of our own time. I see many indications of real life and loyalty to Christ. But this marred the church-life in Thyatira, that the evil influences which were working hurt to the members were allowed to go on. They did not enough contend for abstinence and purity. They allowed a public opinion filled with danger to grow up in the membership. And that very evil, I think, is marring the life of our churches at present. We also are tolerant where we should be intolerant; easy where we should be strict. After our own English fashion, we also "suffer that woman Jezebel to teach and to seduce" Christ's servants. We suffer the vicious public opinion which sustains the drinking customs and feeds drunkenness, and which is the real Jezebel of our day, to continue. And we allow and practise a conformity to the world, which is on one side mere licence and self-indulgence, but on the other a stumbling-block to souls. That is the second symptom of ruin in a church.

III.

It is in the epistle to Sardis the Lord exhibits that next step in the progress of ruin to which churches descend, which have let go their pity for human souls. It is, as we shall see, *Decay of thoroughness in work.*

It is almost a dead church He addresses. Some things remain which may be strengthened; some little shreds and sprigs and roots of life. But with respect to the general and combined life, these are His words :—

"Thou hast a name to live, but thou art dead."

A dead church, with the reputation and standing of a living one! This was its awful state. Like the Church of Rome on the eve of the Reformation; like the Protestant churches at the beginning of the eighteenth century. A dead church! No work, which is the fruit; no truth, which is the root; no love which is the sap and power of life. Everything has gone, or is about to go, in such a church. It has left its first love like Ephesus. It did not take alarm when stumbling-blocks were being scattered along the pathways of the flock. And now—except here and there a humble member all unnoticed, and here and there a little touch of life on the general surface—it has only the reputation of a church. Only the reputation! Almost everything with life in it gone? Almost the whole soul eaten out of it! Only the name remaining!

Our Lord lets us into the secret of this element of ruin by a very simple but suggestive statement, "I have not found thy works perfect before God." There were services, but in His sight imperfectly rendered. Only the show of work; or the work without the love which is its life!

It is not difficult to fancy what such a Church is like. The picture which rises before the mind is that of a full, well-appointed, but dead ministry; respectable but lifeless office-bearers; a fair appearance on the Lord's Day and at all the annual meetings; sermons full of beauty and reports full of eloquence; but underneath all, in the sight of God, the inworking of spiritual death, making its way to the innermost recesses and last retreats of the life of the Church; and everything—missions, benevolence, discipline, worship —hollow, unreal, and dead.

A doing of work, but not a right doing of it. The hands moving as if the work was going forward, but the work not going forward! Necessary sacrifices not offered! Hollowness where there should be strength! Skimming over where there should be careful finishing! In one form or other, a want of thoroughness in the work!

Such a want as there would have been in Paul's work if, when he saw that his eating of idol's meat made his weak brother to stumble, he had refused for that brother's sake to abstain. Such a want as there would be in a mother's work, if when she saw her child in mortal danger, she made no sacrifice, to avert it.

And just this, I think, is the want at present in nearly all the church-work I know which has temperance for its object. It is unthorough. There is this great world of crime, and vice, at her very door; this unexplored wilderness of squalor and indescribable distress, seething with sorrow, with wickedness, with suffering, and smitten to the very soul by drunkenness. The work of the Christian Church in relation to this evil, is nothing less, and can be nothing less, in aim and means used, than the work of Christ Himself. It is just the continuation of Christ's work.

It requires the outgoing of the whole strength of the Church. It implies sympathy, wise planning, sacrifice of time and means, patience, and prayer.

I ask you to consider and place over against this, the actual efforts which the churches in this land are putting forth for the suppression of this evil.

If it were a stagnant pool in the same field with a man's house, and if the foul fogs of it came up and began to penetrate the joints, and loosen the stones, and mildew everything inside, he would surely discover that to bolt the doors and keep the windows shut would be no thorough dealing with the evil. Yet here, in the very field in which the Christian Church has been built, is a pool in our social life, every drop of which carries a power of death in it, and at this moment very nearly all that Churches as such are doing, is, by occasional discipline on its own members, to bolt its doors and keep its windows shut.

We plant Sunday-schools in districts invaded by the evil. We send city missionaries and Bible-women down there to visit and preach. Blessings on the Sunday-school, and all honour to the Bible-women and the missionaries! They do what they can. But I put it to the conscience of those who know that Christ gave Himself to the work, whether all that is an adequate means to use, or a fair proportion of effort to put forth, in such a work?

We hold church meetings about district work, we read fine reports, with extracts from the journals of the missionary and the Bible-woman, and perhaps a touching story about some Sunday-scholar who died happy. Can things like these, can any amount of such things, be any real, effective, human help in the work of delivering poor drunkards from their snare? or any perfect and honest doing of Christ's work towards them?

An earnest spirit arises in the Church; a revival comes; there is a stirring of the household, and the office-bearers and principal people open their doors and come down into the wilderness. But does any serious Christian ever bring himself to believe that it is a thorough doing of this delicate human work to come out from tables on which every luxury in drink which money can purchase has been circulating, and give speeches on temperance to poor labourers, to tramps, and to their untaught wives and children? Or that it is thorough work for people who have not abridged their own liberty in drinking by one solitary sacrifice to stand up in a company of intelligent artisans, men with brains as good as any in the land, and say—the flavour of the speaker's own indulgence still on his breath while he speaks—"Working men, down there, abstinence is a saving virtue for YOU."

Or is it that a thorough doing of this Christian work, with the right hand six days in the week, to be a promoter by actual traffic of drinking, and with the left hand, one day of the seven to be a tract distributor, a Sabbath-school teacher, or a contributor to local charities, or district missions?

Can we mock God? Yet it is really just a mockery of God to put forth such efforts as these for the accomplishment of this work of His, and call them Christian missions to the heathen at home ; or church attempts to abate drunkenness among the poor.

It is profession without reality ; form without power ; reputation without substance. What future remains for churches which act in these ways? There can be, if they do not open their eyes on their errors and shortcomings, and repent, and strengthen the things that remain, but one step lower—and that step has been reached, and is depicted to us in the spiritual condition of those churches of which Laodicea is the type.

IV.

This is the last stage of ruin for a Church. And it is the worst —"neither cold nor hot"—the state in which a Church has become a loathing to Christ. And when has a Church become a loathing to the patient and much-forbearing Christ? It is when it has become self-righteous and proud in its life and ways ; when it is wretched, and yet has no feeling of wretchedness ; when it is lost, and yet has no sense of lostness ; when it has, by its own evil deeds and misdeeds, been abased into the very dust, and yet has no suspicion that it is abased, and no abasement of spirit before God. That is the Church which has become a loathing to Him. A dead, corrupt, lost Church, which says : " I am rich and increased in goods, and have need of nothing."

"Neither cold nor hot!" The love of a living Church to Christ is as coals of fire. It has a vehement flame, and many waters cannot quench it. To glorify Christ, to live for Him, to serve Him, to act in His spirit to the poor outcasts; to go near to them as He did, to do His will towards them, is the one burning wish of such a Church. Its state is that in which life ascends as a flame of fire in His service. And next in well-being to such a state, is that which seems the furthest removed from it, in which Churches realise and mourn over their emptiness, their unworth, their uselessness, their nothingness; feel that they are poor, naked creatures of the holy and great God, unprofitable servants, and out, and justly out, in the cold where His Spirit is not resting.

Paul, flaming along his great path as the Apostle of Christ to the Gentiles, is an illustration of the one state.

The publican in the parable is a picture of the other.

But the Laodicean state of a Church is neither one nor the other of these. It is that in which Gamaliels, Pharisees, diplomatists, and pretentious people abound. Neither hot—burning in loving service to Christ—nor cold, mourning over its misimproved privileges and times, and its consequent want of life, but lukewarm—without feeling of one kind or another—self-satisfied, self-contented, looking down as from some one supreme height of excellence on its human neighbours, on the poor, whom it names *the lower classes— the lapsed classes*—thinking of them as another race, inhabitants of a different and lower world, and comforting itself in its own attainments, in its numbers perhaps, in its financial prosperity perhaps, most commonly in its social position, or some similar outward, and, when life is wanting, altogether unimportant thing.

The tragic thing is that to appearance everything as yet indicates a spiritual state. The material wealth, the outward splendour, everything the Church has gathered in of worldly goods, ranks as so many tokens of prosperity, and the Divine blessing. And so most probably does the fact that its membership is of the better classes, that people of substance adhere to it, that it has social influence in the locality; and in its secret heart it is a consolation to it that it is not a church of poor people, nor an uneducated church, nor a vulgar church, nor a narrow church, like that church in the shabby street which has put temperance on its flag. These are its thoughts about itself. But before God it is, all the while, a very vulgar church, and a church of the very poorest creatures in the world—poor and blind and naked; for it has nothing of Christ at its heart, nothing of Christ in its views, nothing of Christ in its life. A Christless church! A church that does not even sigh or long for Christ—a self-satisfied, proud, dead, blind ruin of a church.

There is no lower stage. All the downward steps have been taken before it could arrive at this. The falling away from love ; the decay of pity, the profession without life ; the want of thoroughness in work ; and now, last and lowest and worst of all, pharisaic self-satisfaction, absolute scorn and heart-hatred of the outcasts, whom it is the Church's first duty to pity and try to bring in ; and thoughts and ways in which God is not at all.

It only needs the arrival of some great crisis in society, some time of public unsettlement and grief, and this will be the subsequent history of such a Church—"The rain descended, and the floods came, and the winds blew and beat upon that house ; and it fell ; and the ruin of that house was great."

I have only two more words to add.

No one will be so uncandid as to suppose that I have been aiming at particular Churches, or very specially at particular classes in the Church. I have spoken as from the heart of the common Christian Church. If, in following the history of possible ruin in a Church, I have had to point to deficiencies, errors, or symptoms of decay in the existing Churches, I have done so not as standing apart from them, far less as standing above them, but always as a partaker both of the blame and the loss they involve.

I ask myself—I desire to press the question on every member of the Christian Church in this country—Can we stand up in the Divine presence and say, We are doing all that His will lays upon us to abate intemperance ? Consider the immense power for good which God has given to His Church. Are we putting forth that power ? I do not hesitate to say, and I do not exaggerate when I say, that the Christian Church has it in its power at any moment to greatly subdue intemperance in the land. It needs but one small sacrifice over all its membership. Let there be the cessation from every Christian home of the drinking customs ; the withdrawal by every Christian man and woman of Christian countenance from these customs. From the highest to the humblest circles let the wine glass and the beer glass be banished from the table, and Christ's people everywhere agree to abstain. Can anybody doubt that a revolution so thorough would make itself felt in the abatement of intemperance in every corner of the land ?

I beseech Christian men to reflect on the grave emergency which drink has brought about in this land. It is not the question of abstinence merely which that emergency is forcing on the Christian conscience. It is also the searching, and nearer question of Christian duty and sacrifice. Shall I take any part in the great Christian burden of sorrow? Shall I put my soul, as Christ did, beneath this huge load of human suffering and sin? By sacrifice of a part, in the spirit of Him who sacrificed the whole, shall I help my poor, weak, fallen brothers to rise? That is the question; and we are each of us bound to settle it in the sight of God.

There arose a great trouble in Israel once, and the cry of it went up to God.

God sent His prophet to see. He found the poor perishing for want of food, ground down by heavy burdens, and despised.

He found the rich lying on beds of ivory, eating the lambs out of the flock, and the calves out of the midst of the stall, with fine music at their feasts, rich wine in their bowls, and precious ointments and perfumes on their persons; but not grieved for " the affliction of Joseph "—the poor people down in the pit.

The brow of the prophet darkened, and these were his words as he turned away:—" Woe unto them that are at ease in Zion!"

This brings me to my closing word. It is the duty of Church members to be repairers of her broken walls.

Next to the great duty of holding fast the elements of life and stability, it is their duty to be restorers, wherever these have been let go.

Our Lord's words in the epistle to Sardis mean this very task, where He says, " Strengthen the things that remain."

All is not ruin at any spot. Some faint germs of life abide. Where there is deadness, we are to work for a revival; where there is error, for enlightenment; and where, as in the case of drunkards, there is the grip of vice, for deliverance.

There are whole fields, and at our very doors, where this last work may be carried on. What is that poor man who shrinks from public view, and creeps through life in the shade? A church ruin: drink cast him from the pulpit into the dust. Who is that, who goes past you in the street, who once, in other days, would have stopped and cordially grasped your hand? Also a church ruin: drink cast him out of the eldership. And who are these, whose footsteps were once music to those who listened for them, whose footsteps are now the subjects of a daily agony and fear? Church ruins also: fathers, husbands, wives, sons, overthrown by drink. Descendants all of them of true Church-members: true members themselves, it may be, in happier times—all of them baptised—all of them ruins of a former life. People like these must be accounted as still belonging to Christ's Church; and as only requiring Christian handling and love to replace them among the living stones in the walls of the house.

And what are those who are termed in the modern phrase, "The lapsed classes in society—the non-church-going population?" Church ruins also. At least two-thirds of our home mission work is a repairing of broken walls. The poor people in our mission districts were, many of them, at one time connected with churches—nearly all with Sabbath-schools. They can turn up the text when you preach to them. They are familiar with the old tunes when you give out a psalm. If you descant on the Saviour's sufferings, or on His sympathies with the poor, the tears will trickle down their cheeks. Ask them, and you will find that they have been baptised. Behind the most of them, and not far behind, is a past in which they went daily to the homely chapel in some country village. Many of them can remember a time when they lived in homes where some form of family worship prevailed. Some of them, perhaps, are longing for such a time to return.

Do not weary, therefore, in this great work, Christian abstainers. Put on new strength from above, and go hopefully into the conflict. You are rebuilding, by every fallen soul you reclaim, the broken walls of Zion.

It is Church ruins you visit when you enter the homes where the victims of intemperance live. Sin, or separation from the old surroundings, or perhaps poverty, or so small a thing to look at as indolence, has broken their old life, and made them the pitiful objects they are. Do not despise them—do not neglect them. Do not say in respect of any of them, "Am I his keeper?" They are fallen, but it is as stones of God's house they are fallen. The Holy Spirit once dwelt in companies of which they may have made a part. Low though they grovel now, in bad ways and in forgetfulness of God, they are all the while stones and the dust of the temple.

O Saviour! O Great Master Builder! *Thou* dost not despise these fallen ones; and over such ruins as even these Thou hast taught us to sing and hope—

> Thou shalt arise, and mercy have
> 　Upon Thy Zion yet;
> The time to favour her is come—
> 　The time which Thou hast set.

> For in her rubbish and her stones
> 　Thy servants pleasure take;
> Yea, they the very dust thereof
> 　Do favour for Thy sake.

www.ingramcontent.com/pod-product-compliance
Lightning Source LLC
Chambersburg PA
CBHW082059070426
42452CB00052B/2739